Individuality  *Books*

DRAGONFLIES
COLORING BOOK

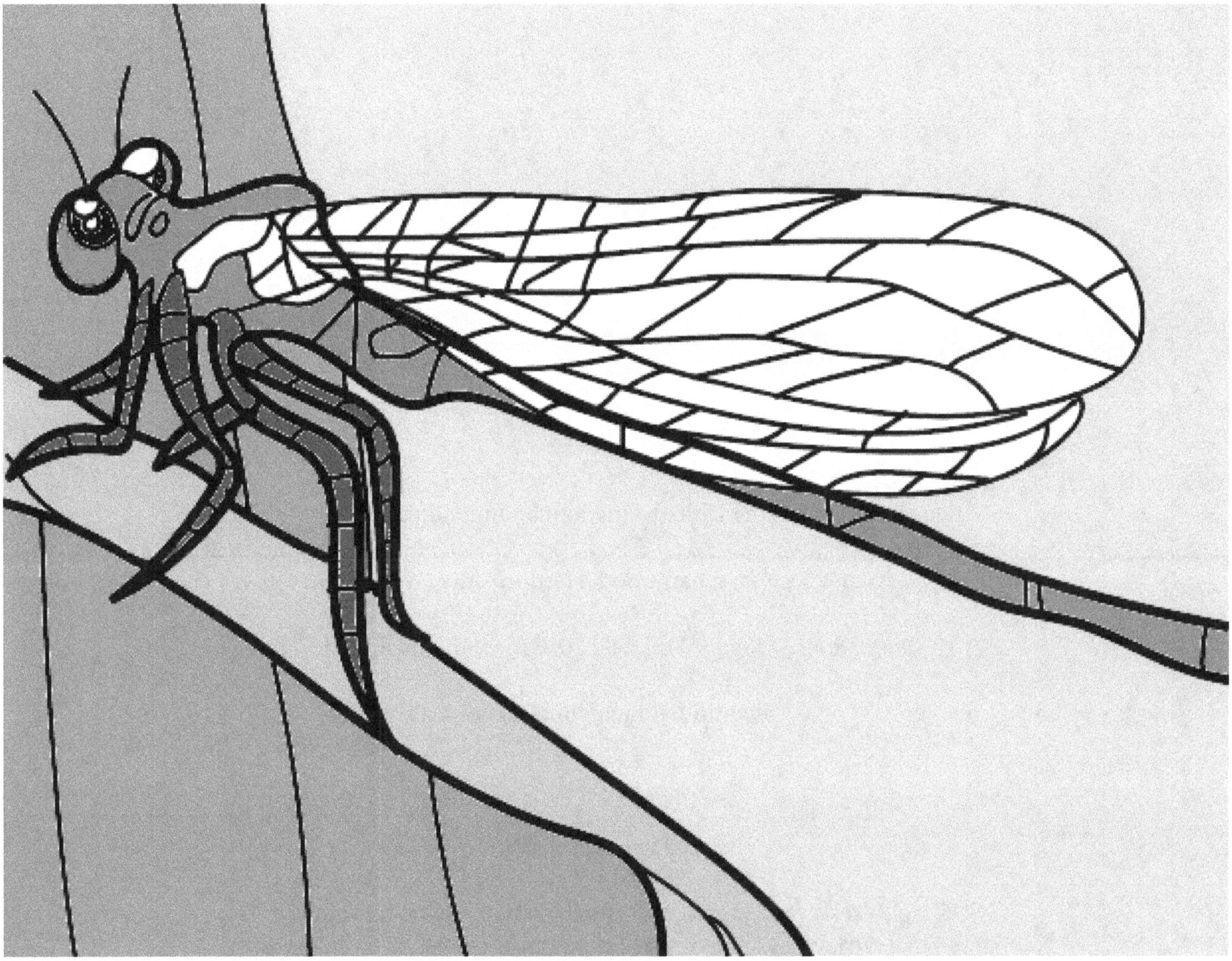

Published in the United Kingdom by Individuality Ltd

7 Ascot Close, Borehamwood, Hertfordshire, WD6 3JH

Illustrations © Kayla Winkfield 2016 for Individuality Ltd

www.individualitybooks.com

Printed in Great Britain

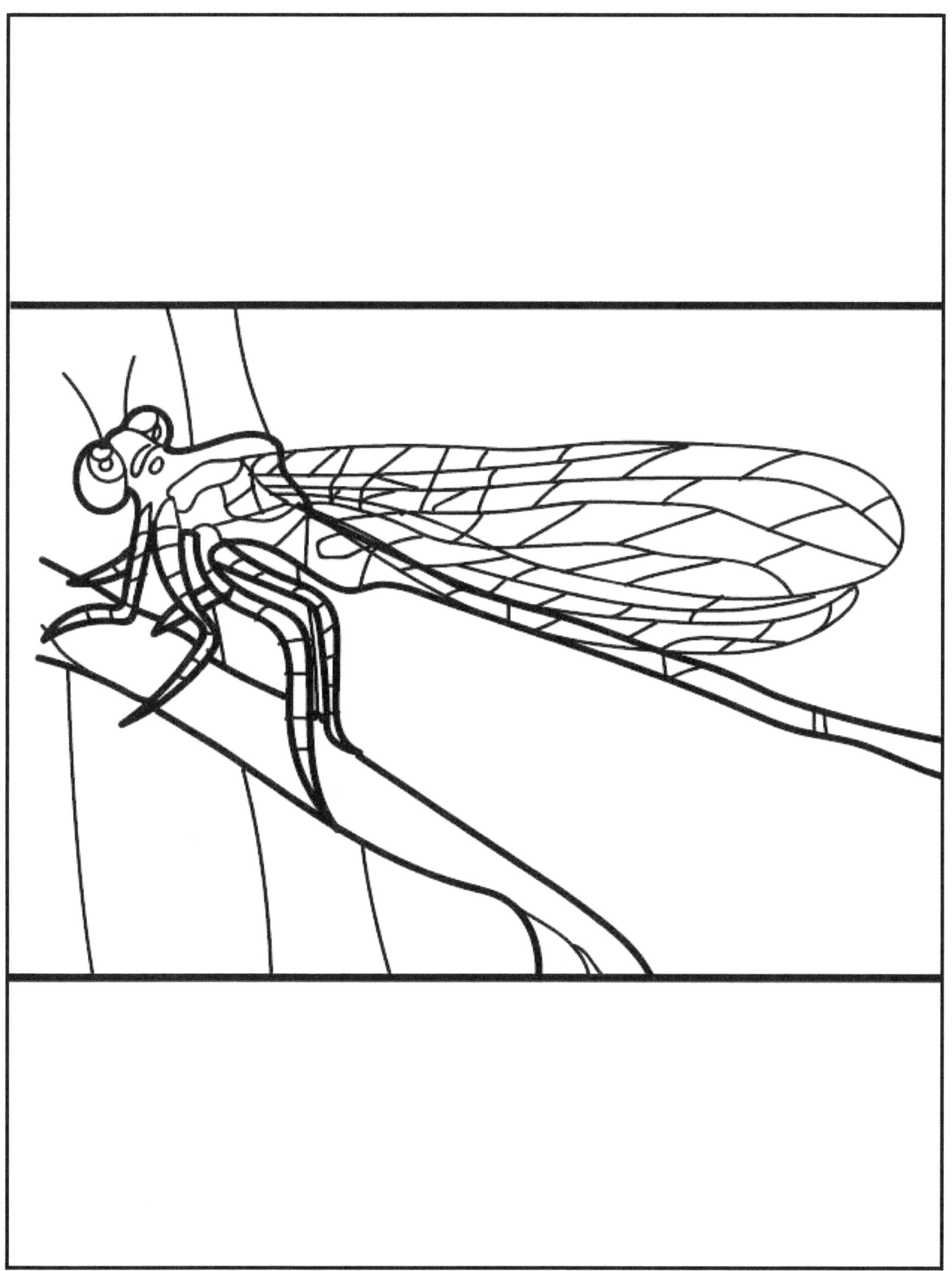

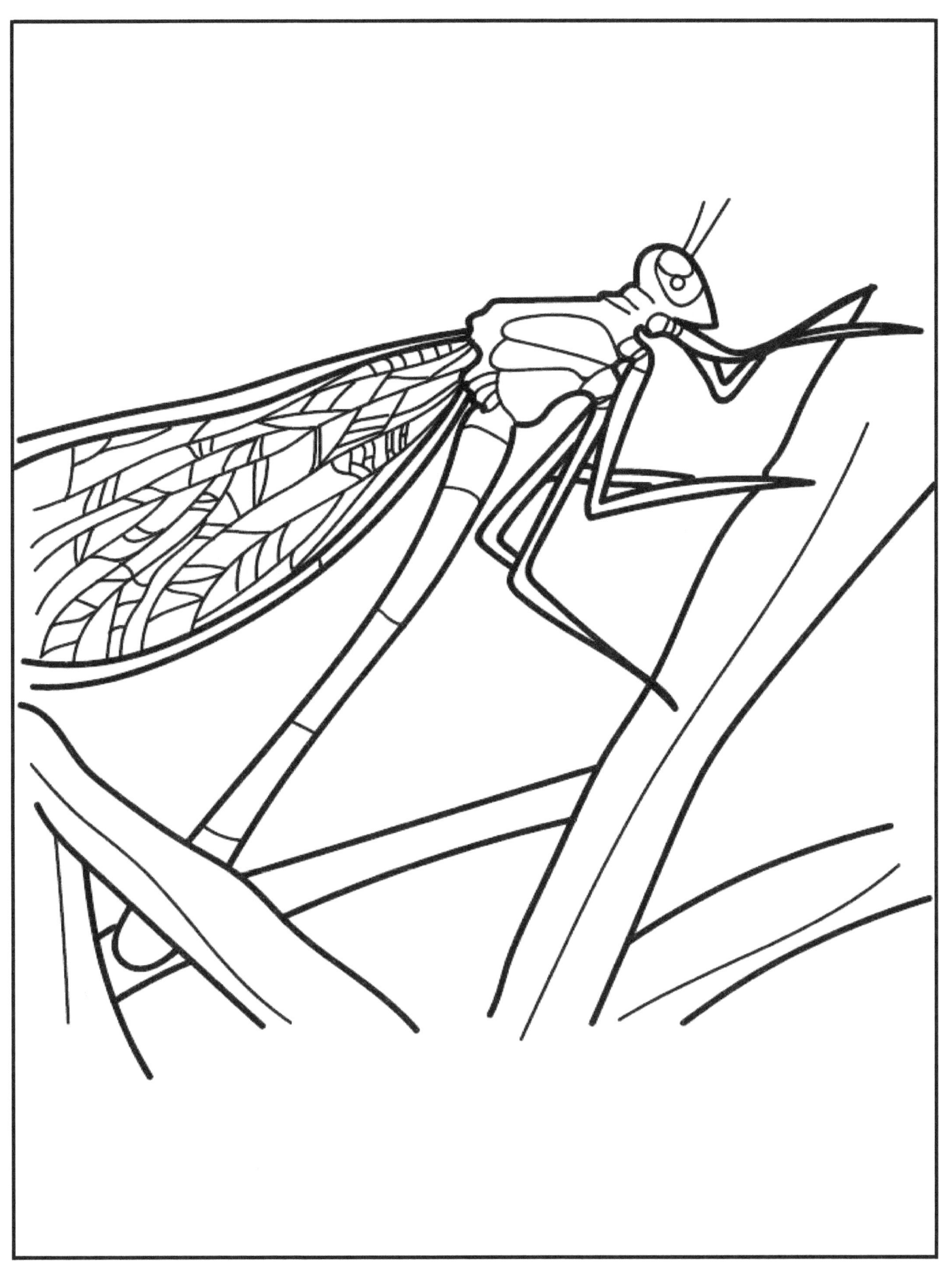

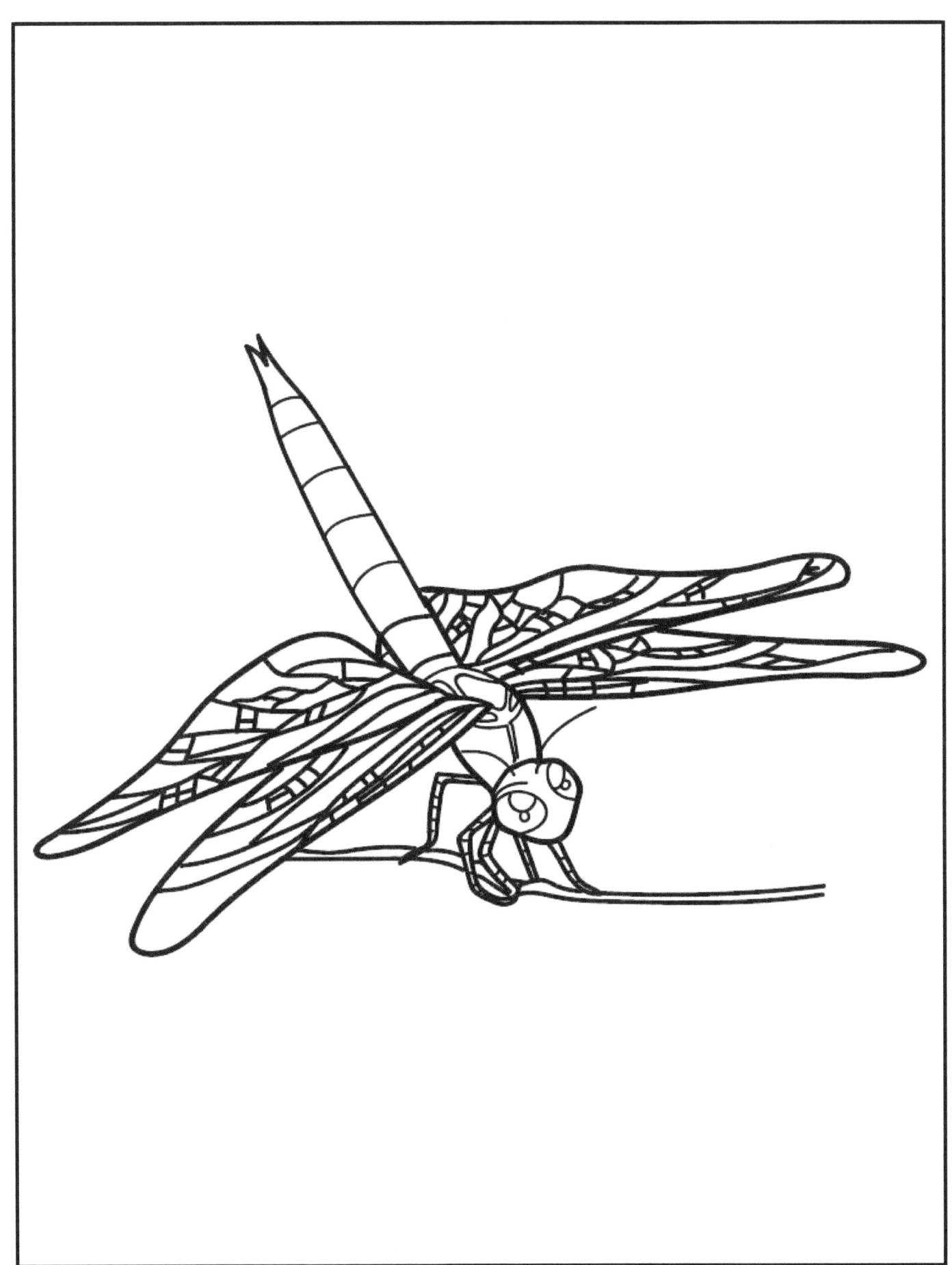

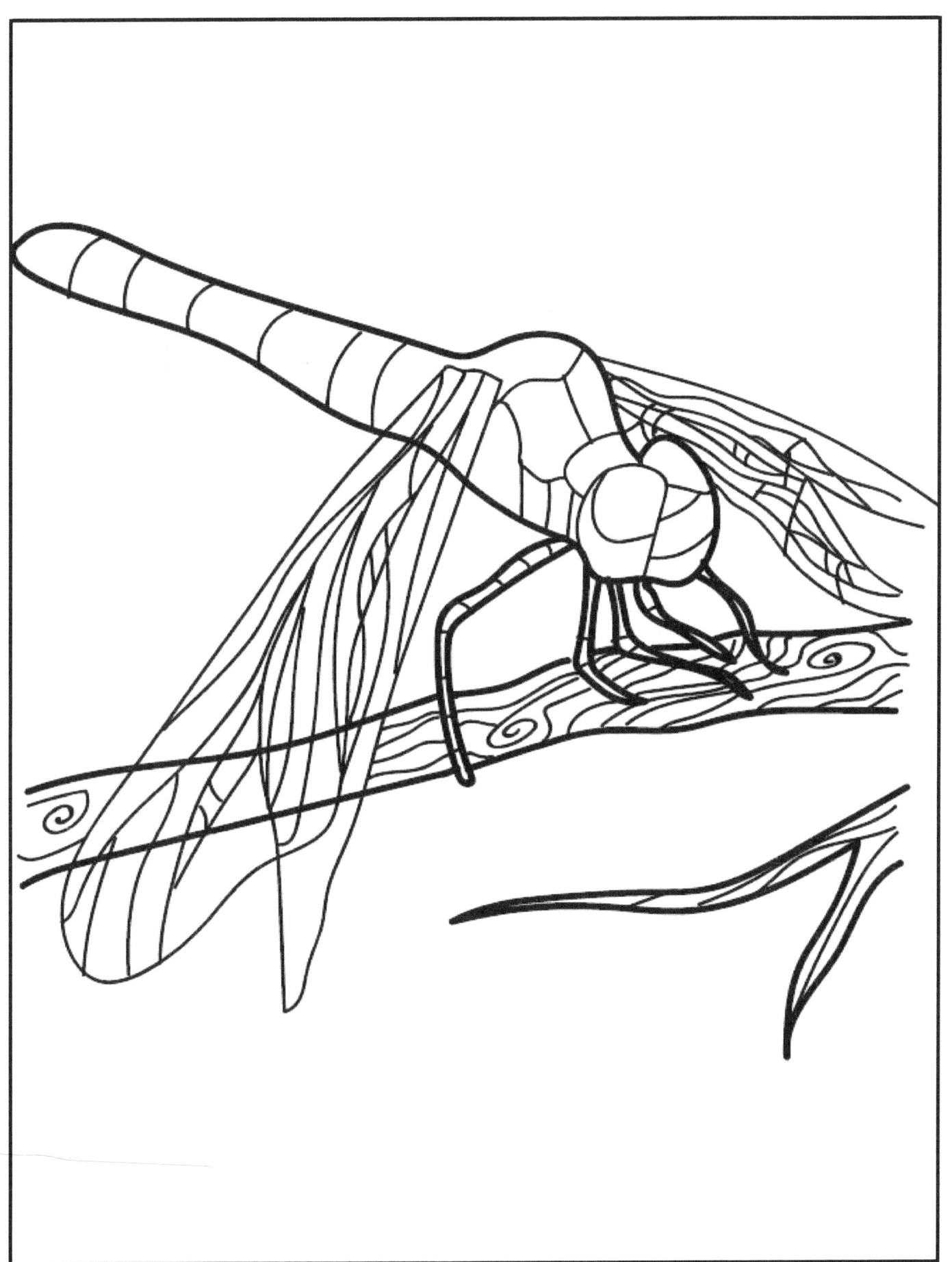

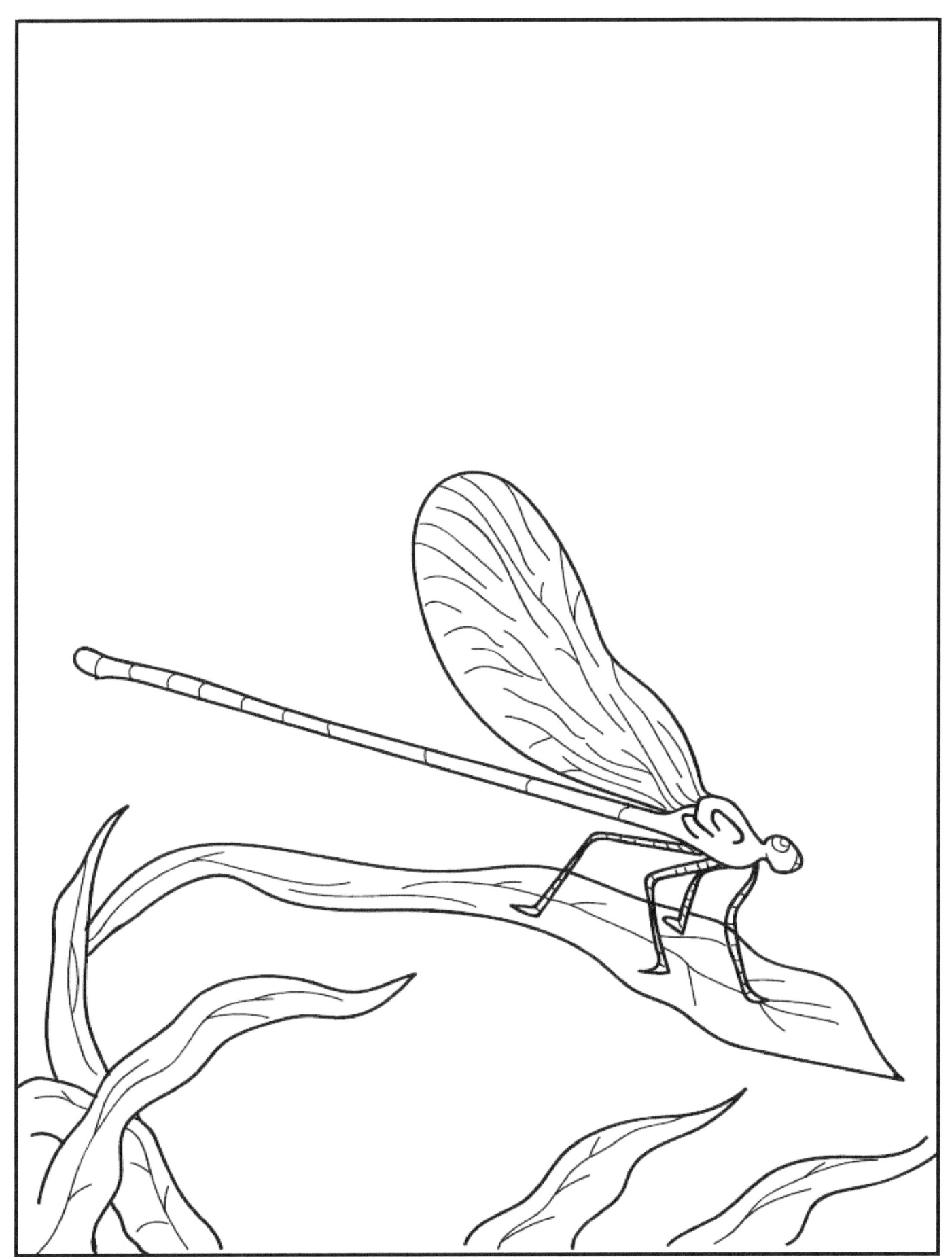

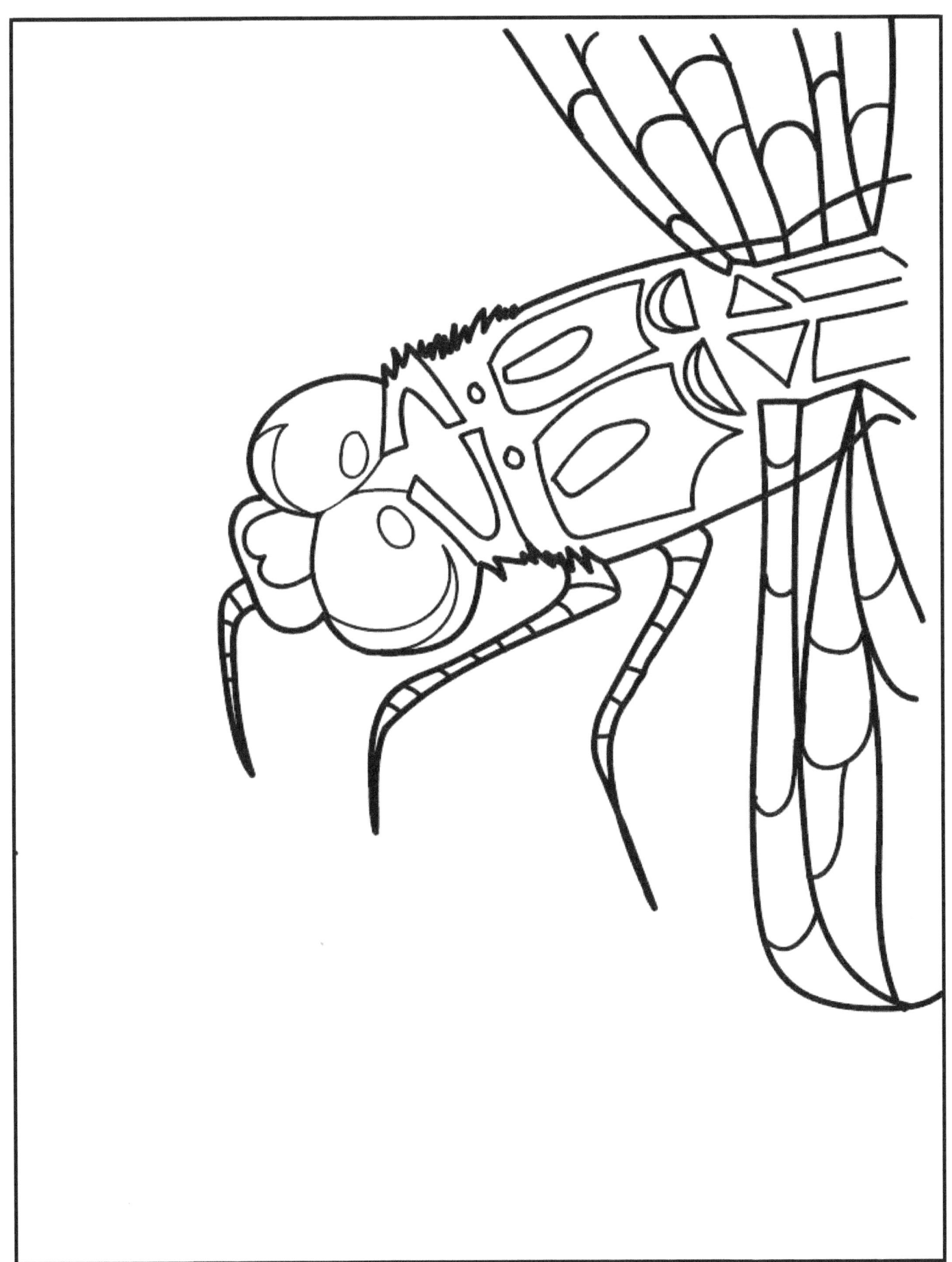

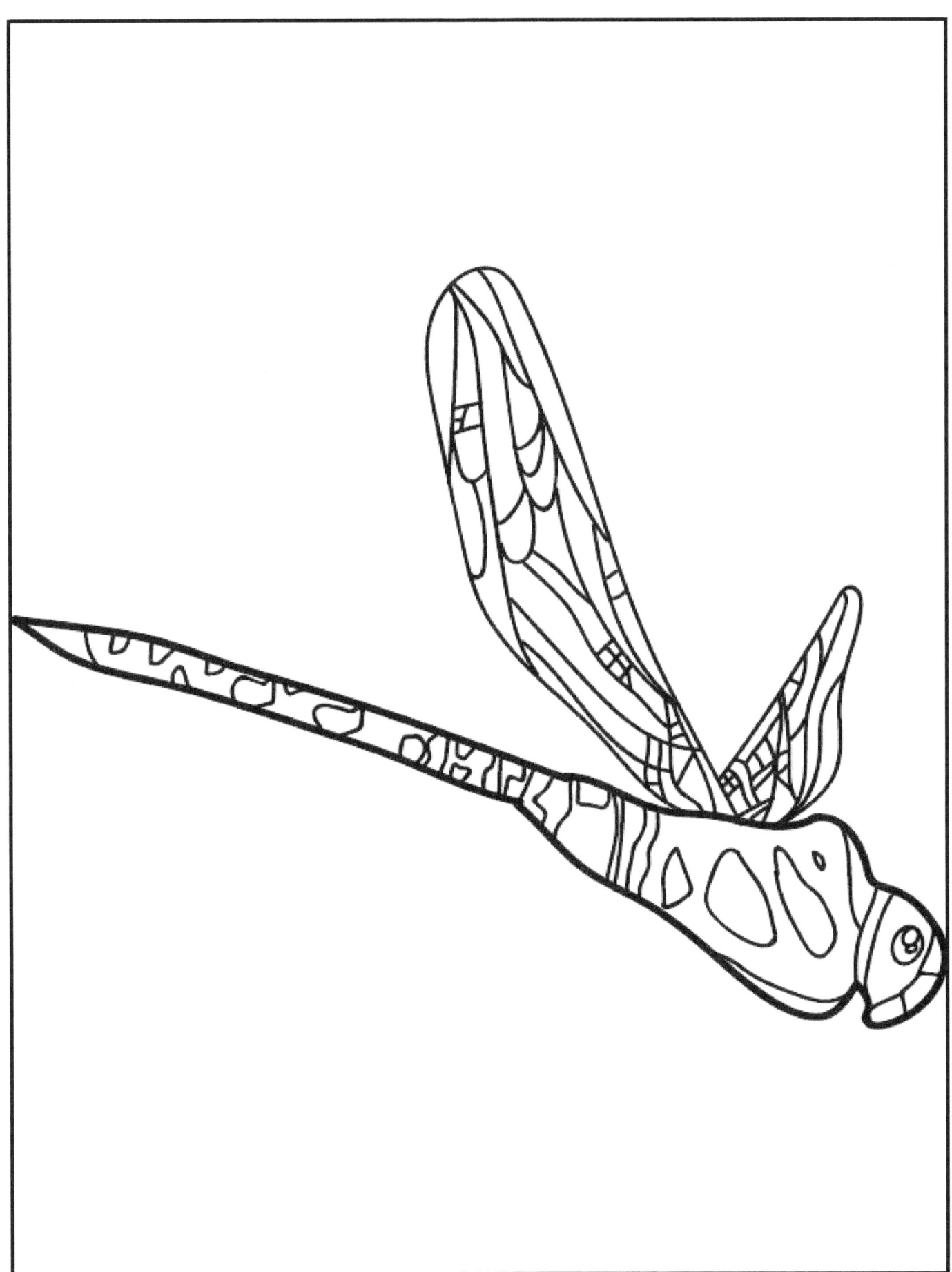

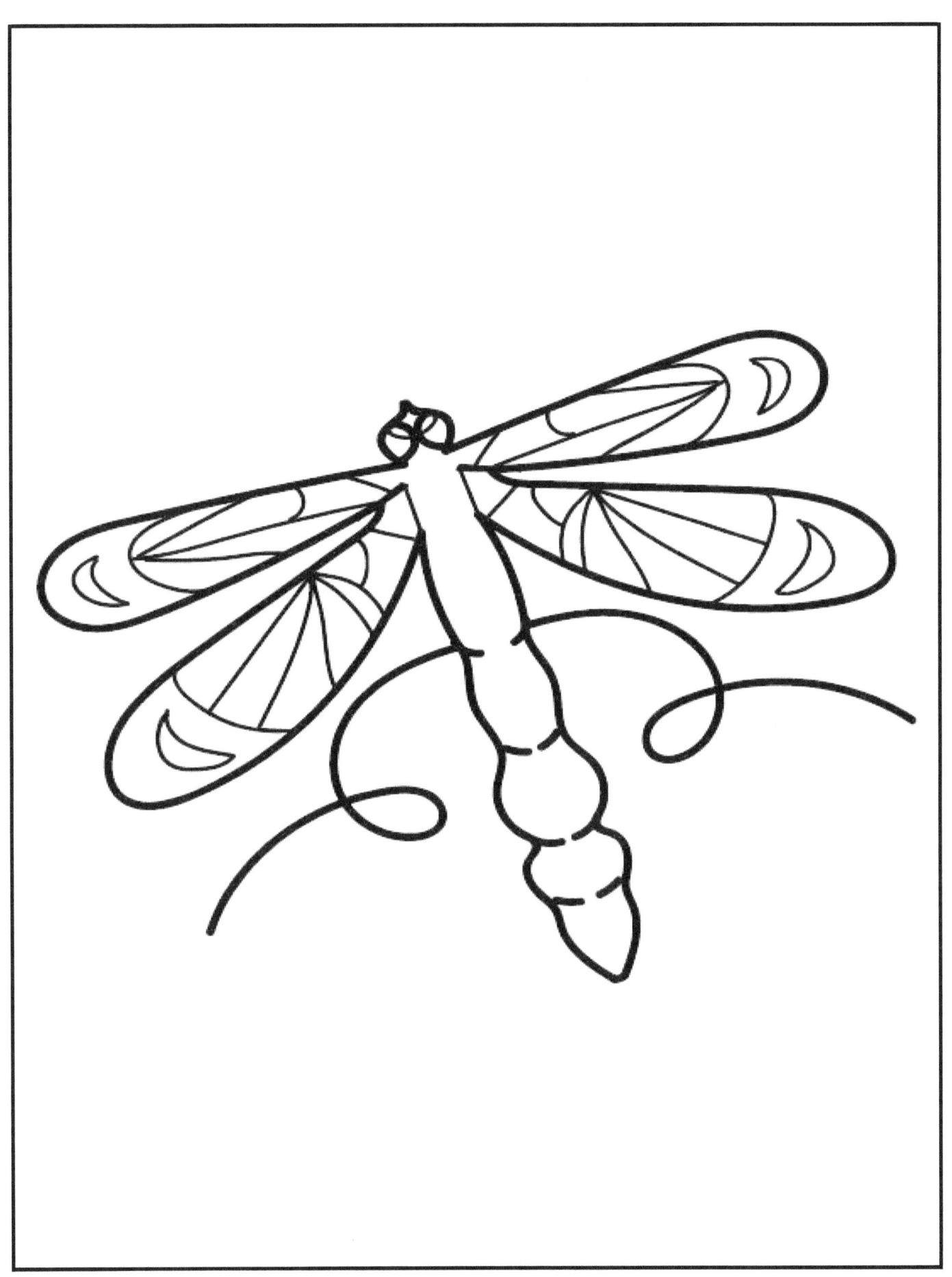

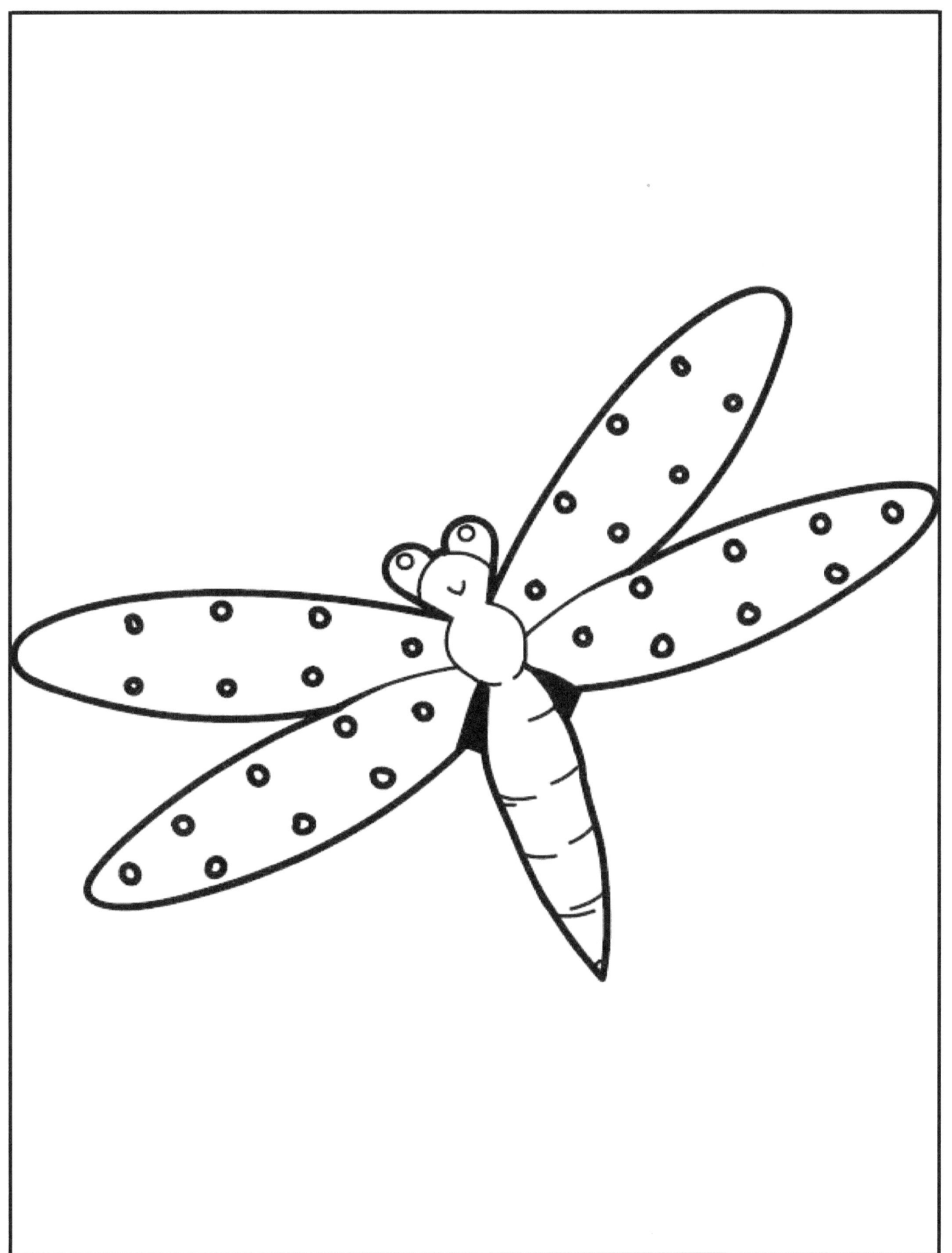